DULAT ISSABEKOV

BONAPARTE'S WEDDING

A COMEDY

London 2022

HERTFORDSHIRE PRESS

Published by HERTFORDSHIRE PRESS Ltd © 2022
e-mail: publisher@hertfordshirepress.com
www.hertfordshirepress.com

BONAPARTE'S WEDDING

Play by DULAT ISSABEKOV

a comedy

English

Translated from Russian by Jonathan Campion
Typeset Alexandra Rey

British Library Catalogue in Publication Data
A catalogue record for this book is available from the British Library
Library of Congress in Publication Data
A catalogue record for this book has been requested

ISBN: 978-1-913356-51-4

BONAPARTE'S WEDDING

A COMEDY

A MAN FROM THE OTHER WORLD

DULAT ISSABEKOV

That was what literary critics and his contemporaries called Dulat Issabekov, when he became a well-known writer of Kazakhstan. When he was just over a year old, Dulat fell seriously ill, and died – or so they thought. The child's body was put out into a cold corridor prior to its burial the following day. Everything was ready for the funeral – the long shirt the child was to be buried in and the meal for the wake after the burial. Then all of a sudden an old lady neighbour, who had been entrusted with the task of handing the infant's body to the grave-diggers, let out a frantic scream. It turned out that the child was still alive, and not just alive, but laughing, after catching sight of the old woman. This was how Dulat returned from the other world just an hour before his funeral was due to start. This happened in 1943, exactly a year after his father had been killed at the Battle of Stalingrad. The writer was to recall: "We were children then, but robbed of our childhood. Our fathers had been lost at the front and our childhood in villages far away from it". Dulat's mother died on the very day he joined the Communist Youth League aged 14. After that his elder brothers and sisters assumed responsibility for him and he went to a boarding

school for orphans in the town of Arys. After leaving school, Dulat became an apprentice fitter in railway communications. In 1961 he gained a place in the philology faculty of the Kazakh State University, from which he graduated in 1966. When Dulat was a student in his final year, a collection of his stories and novellas, entitled "Beket", was published. It was to prove a sensation at the time. The response from critics and readers was a rapturous one. Since 1996 - Member of Kazakhstan Social Democratic Party "Aul". 1966 -1967 - the editor of the Kazakh Radio, served in the Soviet Army. 1971 – Head of "Zhuldyz" Journal ; 1973 - Head of the editorial publishing "Zhalyn"; 1983 - Editor-repertoire of the editorial board of the Ministry of Culture of the Kazakh SSR; 1989 - chief editor of political books; 1991 - General Director of Radio and Television of the Kazakh SSR television. 1992 - Director of the publishing house "Zhazushy." 1998 - Director of the Kazakh Research Institute of Culture and Art. Dulat has always actively engaged in social activities. He is a member of Arts Council of Kazakhfilm, a member of the political council of the party "Aul", a member of the executive committee of the Kazakh PEN Club. The first story by Dulat Issabekov "The Way" was included in a collection of stories of writers of Kazakhstan called "Contemporary" in 1963, when he was still at university. In the same year, the most popular newspaper of the time, "Leninshil zhas" published his story "Shoyynkulak" and one day, as they say, he woke up a famous young writer.

Literary critics unanimously celebrated his success and unique talent. His stories "Beket", "Gauhar tas", "Notes from a lodger", "Restless Days", "Line of Communication", "Wormwood", "On the sidelines", "Silent", "You did not know war," "Transit passenger" and dozens of others were published one after the other in the press and as a separate book. And in 1980 came the publication of his novel "Kargyn" ("Confusion"), which to this day is very popular, especially among young people. His works "Father's house", "New home in the old house" and "Transit passenger" were published in book form by the Moscow publishing house "Soviet Writer". The novel "Kargyn" "Atamura" (2012); Collection (in 7 volumes). "Atamura", 2012; "Gauhar tas", "Atamura", 2012; Collection of translated works, "Audarma" 2012. Movies of D.Issabekov: "Gauhar tas "(1975); "Wormwood" (1994); "Destiny" (based on the story "Tirshilik", 1998); "Munlyk-Zarlyk" animated film, the studio ("Zhebe") (2010); "Bird of Happiness" - the agency "Khabar" (2011); "The Lottery" - Film studio "Kazakhfilm" S.Aymanov (2012); "The old sister" - TV series. Today Dulat Issabekov has dozens of novellas to his name, around forty short stories and a novel entitled "The Revolt". He has also written over twenty works for the stage. Issabekov's works have been published and republished in Moscow on several occasions. Some of his novellas and stories have been translated into German, Hungarian, Czech and Chinese. Plays by this writer are performed in theatres throughout Kazakhstan. They have also been staged in Turkey, St Petersburg,

Omsk, Sofia (Bulgaria), Tajikistan and Bashkortostan. In 2012 a whole international festival was devoted exclusively to his work under the title "The World of Issabekov". Since 2014 his play "The Transit Passenger" has became known in the UK.

Dulat Issabekov was the first writer to be awarded the State Prize of Independent Kazakhstan, the prize of Kazakhstan's PEN Club and the Platinum Prize of the independent organization "Tarlan". Feature films have been made of Issabekov's works "Gaukhar Tas", "Sagebrush", "Far and Away", "Lottery", "Baluan sholak", and also a documentary about his life and work entitled "The World of Issabekov" (2012). In 2014 he received the International Chingiz Aitmatov Award in the House of Lords, British Parliament for his achievements in Literature.

HONOURS: Winner of the M. Auezov Writers' Union (1985, for the play "Muragerler" (Heirs)); Awarded the Order of "Kurmet" (2002); 2009 - the play "Munlyk-Zarlyk" was awarded a grant from the Ministry of Culture and Information; 2010 - the play "Zhauzhyrek" won the Grand Prix in the competition "Tauelsizdik tolgauy"; 2008 - the play "Endi қayttik? .." (What shall we do ?) has been awarded a grant from the Ministry of Culture and Information; Awarded the Order of "Astana" (2008); Awarded the medal of "Leo Tolstoy", Russia (2012); 2012 - D. Issabekov was awarded the Diploma of the National Academy of Science. Awarded the Order of "Barys"

(2012); 2012 - President of Kazakhstan Nursultan Nazarbayev congratulated Dulat Issabekov by special letter.

Dulat Issabekov teaches film courses at the T. Zhurgenov Academy of Arts. He also edits the magazine "Madeniet."

REVIEW

Weddings have the capacity to bring great joy or invoke human fragility. With Bonaparte's Wedding Dulat Issabekov sets the bar high for dark comedy, with Kazakh traditions being challenged and a family in turmoil over a long-kept secret. Unfortunately secret's have a habit of being discovered..

A sense of foreboding is felt at the outset of the play with the congregating villagers lamenting "Now we've got the stench of this scandal on us, do we at least have the right to have our say about it?" This is in contrast with the innocent youthful exclamations preceding it of a young boy telling the village a Wedding shall be taking place very soon of his brother Bonaparte.

Unconventional and unrepenting seems to be one of the many surprises of Bonaparte's Wedding in the form of Bonaparte's parents Father Abdashim and Mother Ultugan, who very much echo their liberal son Bonaparte with their attitudes. With a carefree and measured approach to the potentially disastrous situation they are faced with about their soon to be married son, it is fascinating the quarrelling that takes place by judgemental Uncle's Auganbek and Ispanali as a result. Their referring of Bonaparte as an "infidel" is a huge insult to a muslim man, but the Uncle's old-fashioned views are often a cause of great humour with it's shock value and directness.

The play is one that relies on epic speeches and seem to be spoken from every character's mouth apart from Bonaparte, with Ultugan reminding her Uncle Ispanali he once told her "We mustn't let our horizons be narrowed by nationalism" because of pure criticism of his French name alone. The humour throughout is only heightened by the fact everyone has an opinion on the play's protagonist and his Wedding except him.

Bonaparte's Wedding is an extremely witty and intelligent look at tradition and redemption, showing just how complicated life can become when metaphorically the old and modern customs encounter each other face to face.

Francesca Mepham,
Theater critic, writer (UK).

REVIEW

'Bonaparte's Wedding' has been described as 'caustic' but anyone who has spent time in rural central Asia will see the imagery that Dulat Issabekov paints through his magical comedy play. The characters are all too familiar in every yurt community and the political and social changes that have occured over the past thirty years are picked out thread by thread. The overall 'tapestry' is more made of 'felt' that woven and if you close your eyes you can visualise the scenes, interiors and even the clothing people wear.

A comedic yet serious issue has the potential to derail the arranged marriage and the resulting involvement of village elders and busybodies leads to witty and insightful dialogue from colourful characters that are just waiting for a comedy actor's portrayal. It has the feel of a British Sitcom and even Monty Python and I can't wait to see it performed on the stage!

Gareth Stamp
Chairman Eurasian Creative guild

REVIEW

"Before Perestroika we had atheism"…A fascinating, humorous snapshot of post-Soviet village Kazakh life. Skillfully combining absurdity, cultural norms, Isabekov sets out a leftfield platform to joke on oft felt issues of extreme sensitivity. And what with Bonaparte, Roosevelt, and even Ho Chi Min offering naming rights to the locals we are in for a giant dollop of the ridiculous posing as the norm. Clearly a writer at the top of his game, delighting in the foibles that a newly claimed freedom exposes!

Warren Wills
Australian Director, composer, pianist

CHARACTERS:

BONAPARTE
AUGANBEK
ISPANALI
ABDASHIM
ULTUGAN
AKSAKAL RAT *[An aksakal is the name given in Kazakhstan to a male elder, traditionally the leader of the village]*
CHAPAI
ROLLAN
TASBOLAT
KASHPIROVSKY

Cheerful music.

A young boy is running around the stage. The boy is Chapai – Bonaparte's younger brother.

– Hurrah! It's decided! In a month Bonaparte will bring a bride into the house!

Everyone is invited to the wedding! Come along! Share our joy with us! There will be a huge celebration in our house next month! Come along! Come along!

The cheerful music and dancing continues.

***

From two sides of the stage, people of various ages walk into the centre, looking worried. They come together, whisper about something, then quickly separate.

Some of the remarks can be heard above the concerned whispers. The women place their hands over their faces, clearly appalled by something shameful.

There is a general commotion.

What a disgrace! How are we going to look people in the eye now? How awful!

The real shame is still to come! If their parents find out about this travesty then there will be hell to pay!

I'd rather die than walk around with such shame!

We will never hear the end of this, as long as we are alive!

Why did this have to happen to us! What a disgrace! It's awful!

Oh my, what are their parents going to say when they find out about this?

Now we've got the stench of this scandal on us, do we at least have the right to have our say about it? Can't we object?

Oh my-my! There will be nothing left, we'll all be thrown to the wolves!

*** The same boy is running again.

Bonaparte is getting married! The wedding is in a month! Everyone is invited! Come along! Share our joy with us!

ISPANALI. What is your name, boy?

CHAPAI. Chapai.

ISPANALI. And are you really preparing for a wedding?

CHAPAI. Yes! I have already written you an invitation.

AUGANBEK. Oh have you indeed? And have you written one for me as well?

CHAPAI. No, I haven't got round to yours yet. Here's your invitation…

(Chapai gives the invitation to Ispanali).

ISPANALI. Is your father at home?

CHAPAI. He was there when I left.

AUGANBEK. In that case run home as fast as you can. Make sure your father and mother don't go anywhere. We will come to see them in a while. There is something urgent to discuss.

CHAPAI. Uncle Ispanali, uncle Auganbek, are you upset about something?

Are you both alright?

ISPANALI. We will tell you when we get there. Now run home...

CHAPAI.   I still have a lot of invitations to –...

AUGANBEK. *(Interrupting).* When someone tells you to run, you run. You're too smart for your own good. You'll still have time to hand out your invitations. That's if there will be a wedding to invite anyone to! *(The boy runs away).*

***

Bonaparte's home. In the house are his father Abdashim, his mother Ultugan, Auganbek, Ispanali and the village aksakal Rat. This is the village's 'emergency committee', which gathers whenever there is an extraordinary event. Everyone is looking very serious, sitting with crossed arms and furrowed brows.

RAT. Well everyone, let's begin. Where are those two idiots? Call them here!

Abdashim enters with Ultugan. They walk gloomily, with their heads bowed guiltily.

Eh, you, you pair of sinners! Is it true that your offspring, who is planning to get married in a month, was never circumcised?

ABDASHIM. Well... um... you see....

RAT. I'll ask you again: is it true or is it not true that he wasn't circumcised? Speak, don't be embarrassed...

ABDASHIM. If that's what people are saying then it must be true. How should we know, how can we check, do you expect us to inspect him?

RAT. Oh, you odious cretin! Did you hear what he's suggesting?

Apostate!

ISPANALI. Eh, Abdashim! If you don't know which of your six sons are circumcised and which aren't, evil spirits must have come over you, wouldn't you say?

ABDASHIM. It was all just a blur... I had too much work, there was no time... It slipped my mind...

AUGANBEK. You're not the only one who has work to think about. None of us are free from it either...

ISPANALI. And our aksakal, Rat, has eleven sons and nineteen grandsons – and he didn't forget about any of them. Isn't that right, aksakal?

RAT. Heaven forbid I could ever be so careless!

ISPANALI. Does this infidel think that the six sons that God gave him are a burden on him? And aksakal Rat, isn't he the one who once upon a time raised six hundred sheep on the kolkhoz *[Soviet collective farm]*, and knew each of them like the back of his hand? He knew which of the ewes were pregnant and which weren't. Isn't that right, aksakal?

RAT. Yes, of course! Of course!

ISPANALI. Did you hear that? Six hundred sheep! And you've only got six sons and still can't keep track of them!

ABDASHIM. Yes, but those were sheep. A person isn't an animal...

AUGANBEK. Yes, exactly: a person isn't an animal. But the two of you are! ULTUGAN. Me as well?

AUGANBEK. Yes, both of you. I don't see any justification for your behaviour.

ULTUGAN. My dear aunt and uncle, don't you remember the day I received a gold medal from the president himself? And don't you remember the time when we were all gathered around the dastarkhan *[a dining table laid out for a special occasion]*, and you praised us in front of the guests? Oh, my precious relatives, what has changed since then?

AUGANBEK. *(A little slower)*. Hmm... yes, perhaps I did give you some praise.

But opinions of people can always change. And how can I not change my mind, after hearing such shameful news?

ISPANALI. Well, well! Instead of admitting their mistakes, these idiots are putting all the blame on us!

AUGANBEK. Exactly! And after abandoning your children to the whims of fate, what have you been doing ever since?

ABDASHIM. Why do you say we abandoned them? No one abandoned them – they didn't raise themselves...

ISPANALI. You know what you can do with your "raising"! No, how on earth did you manage to forget

that one of your children hadn't been circumcised? It'd be better if you told us that!

ABDASHIM. As you know, just as our children were starting to grow up, Perestroika began...

ISPANALI. And did you do anything worthwhile before Perestroika?

ABDASHIM. Before Perestroika we had atheism. You said yourself that circumcision was a thing of the past. You went after the mullahs who still performed them. It even got to a point where boys who had been snipped weren't allowed in the Komsomol [*Communist youth organisation*]. Aksakal Rat, give us your sacred word: isn't it true that it was forbidden?

RAT. Eh, is it really worth digging up the past? They did all sorts of filthy things to us – Heaven forbid we have to go through it again!

ISPANALI. But it is your fault that you so dutifully followed every order from above. The authorities gave us orders, and we gave you orders. You should have followed your grandfathers' ways, and not blindly listened to orders that did so much harm to our nation!

AUGANBEK. Exactly! Muslims whose faith was strong didn't let anyone push them off the righteous path, even when they were threatened with the sharp spear of atheism. Even the secretary of the district committee, Esentai, brought all three of his children to aksakal Rat one night, under cover of darkness. And why? To have them circumcised. Isn't that right, aksakal?

RAT. Eh… well... sometimes ... it is the work of God…

ULTUGAN. They say that when Esentai himself was a small boy, it was our respected aksakal who made a Muslim of him....

ISPANALI. Stop it! It isn't good to spread dirty rumours.

AUGANBEK. *(Laughing)*. Oh, my poor uncle! Is there anyone in this village you haven't seen? Even the secretary of the district committee...

ISPANALI. Stop your chattering! Abdashim, where is your infidel son?

RAT. Careful! You mustn't call a Muslim an infidel!

ISPANALI. And what must we call a man who wasn't circumcised? Call your son here – we'll see what he has to say for himself.

VOICES. Call Bonaparte! Get Bonaparte here!

ISPANALI. Bonaparte! And anyway, how could you give that scatterbrain son of yours such a ridiculous name? Couldn't you think of anything more suitable?

ULTUGAN. Oh my dear uncle, wasn't it you who gave him that name, when we were all welcoming him into the world? You know, there is a country called France, and they, like us, have a lot of brave men. If you go there you'll see that there are lots of surnames like Conrad, Naimann, Aragon. If the French, out of respect for us, can use Kazakh names for their surnames, then why can't we name our children after their nation's heroes? Wasn't it you who used to shout that "We mustn't let our horizons be narrowed by nationalism"?

ISPANALI. That was the policy of the time! My father and mother also gave me a regal name: Ispanali! And that one they named Auganbek.

ULTUGAN. You called my third baby Ho Chi Minh! By the time we applied for a passport for him, we only just managed to convince them to change it to the Kazakh 'Koishiman'. These days there are all

sorts of half-forgotten leaders and relics from past eras. Chapai, Shchors! And where is Bonaparte?

VOICES: He's coming, he's coming!

A tall, gangly man enters the house. Here it isn't by any means necessary to describe him in great detail. This can be left to the director, and depends on the resources that the theatre has. The most important thing is that the character has an air of comedy about him.

AUGANBEK. In front of you stands His Excellence, Bonaparte, son of Abdashim!

ISPANALI. Listen here boy, why don't you hurry when people call for you? And where have you been, you have caused these good people all sorts of pains…

BONAPARTE. We are strengthening the material and technical basis for communism.

VOICES. What did he say? What is that nincompoop talking about?

BONAPARTE. I said I have been busy at work.

AUGANBEK. Ah, then why didn't you say so! If the material and technical basis for communism depends on the work you do, then there is no hope for it! And what do you do there?

BONAPARTE. Roosevelt's car got stuck in a ditch, and Churchill and I are trying to haul it out with a tractor.

AUGANBEK. Oh you idiot, are you in your right mind?

BONAPARTE. Well, it was you who raised me…

Bektur enters with a newspaper in his hands. Without paying attention to anyone, his eyes still glued to the newspaper, he walks straight through the group, dividing them into two parts.

BEKTUR. Roosevelt! Churchill! Bonaparte! Chapai! Shchors! Kazakh simpletons, you can't even name your children properly! Ispanali! Iranbek! Irakbek! Hahaha!

He leaves.

ISPANALI. Where did that odd man come from?

AUGANBEK. Who invited him? Why did he come, why did he leave?

ABDASHIM. Don't you know who that was? Wasn't that Bektur, the village poet?

ULTUGAN. That poor young man… He used to work on building sites. He became a pretty good bricklayer, until last year when a brick landed on his head. The poor lad, since then he's been a poet. He walks around just like that…

ISPANALI. Let's not get distracted. Bonaparte, Your Excellency, how are you feeling, are you ready to take a wife?

BONAPARTE. I am!

AUGANBEK. My foot he's ready!

BONAPARTE. And what do you need to be ready? I'm in healthy mind, all my organs work, and you've already given the girl's family half of the dowry. I've seen the girl herself twice. I like her. And she doesn't mind being friends with me either. What else do you need?

ISPANALI. Just listen to what comes out of his mouth! What else do you need?

I'll tell you what else you need!

BONAPARTE. What?

ISPANALI. What, he's asking! Eh, Auganbek, tell that moron what else you need to take a wife... You don't have any shame – you've never had any!

AUGANBEK. Why are we tiptoeing around the issue? Why don't we just cut to the chase? All your relatives are making plans for your wedding, and you haven't even been circumcised. Is this true?

BONAPARTE. Well how should I know?

ISPANALI. Oh, you…! And who do you think is going to know, if not you? Me?

BONAPARTE. Well, my parents...

AUGANBEK. *Eurgh!* Are you hearing this nonsense? His parents! Your parents don't have a clue about anything. Their brains went soft years ago!

ABDASHIM. Eh, Auganbek! Do you think you can just say out loud anything that comes into your head? It's as if you think you're so clever, and we're stupid!

AUGANBEK. Then why aren't you managing your son better?! What else do you expect us to say about this?

ULTUGAN. Listen, uncle! Seeing as our aksakal is present, I wanted to do the polite thing and stay silent. But you're taking us for some kind of dunces – not letting us speak a word of our own, and treating us like imbeciles. I, praise God, brought six sons and three daughters into this world. And at each of our meetings, you and your activist wife order people to "support the wish of the president to bring the number of Kazakhs to twenty million". You may be giving the orders, but it's us who are giving birth! If we're losing our minds then there is a reason for it. While you are spending all your time fighting to get heating into our homes, we don't want to be there with only one child.

ISPANALI. Well said, auntie, that's shown him! *(To Auganbek).* She is talking about you too, beaurocrat! Maybe now you might stop blowing hot air and start actually doing something. Haha!

RAT. Stop this idle chatter! We have an issue to discuss!

AUGANBEK. Then let's get to the issue. So it appears you don't know yourself whether you have been circumcised or not? You really are a simpleton! It doesn't take a genius to work it out…

ISPANALI. Eh, Auganbek! What are we doing getting cross at each other like this? Can't he just go outside, take a look and come back?

AUGANBEK. But of course! Why didn't we think of this sooner? Bonaparte! Get up and come with me! We're going to go and see something!

Auganbek and Ispanali clumsily drag Bonaparte out.

CHAPAI. Dad, Mum, is Bonaparte not going to get married?

ABDASHIM. Just wait a little, son. It all depends on what your uncles decide when they come back.

CHAPAI. Aksakal Rat, please let Bonaparte have his wedding. I have already given invitations to half of the village. What will we tell them?

RAT. Patience, my boy, patience…

CHAPAI. I have seen Bonaparte's bride. She's such a pretty girl! There was a beauty contest and she was named Miss District…

ABDASHIM. Then we're in big trouble…

CHAPAI. Why?

ABDASHIM. Because if a girl who they called Miss District hears about this, we'll be the laughing stock of the whole region.

ULTUGAN. Do you think this backstreet beauty queen was brought to us on gilded lilies? I saw her last year at a gathering somewhere. There's nothing special about her – she's an ordinary Kazakh girl, with dark skin and a flat nose. There's a rumour going around that her father spent most of his savings to buy her that title.

CHAPAI. That's not true! People only say that because they're jealous. She's actually a very beautiful girl!

ULTUGAN. So what if she's pretty? My son is handsome as well...

Auganbek and Ispanali enter.

AUGANBEK. We have our answer...

ISPANALI. He definitely hasn't been circumcised.

RAT. And where is he now?

AUGANBEK. He's gone back to work. As he was leaving, he said that if he didn't get that girl he would hang himself.

ABDASHIM. What? Why was he talking about hanging himself?

ULTUGAN. Because of his bride? To hell with her! No bride will ever be worthy of my little boy!

Ultugan runs away, her head in her hands.

ISPANALI. But no-one knew anything about this matter until today! Why did they have to make a problem out of it? And why today, of all days?

ABDASHIM. What problem?

ISPANALI. What problem? It's like you're mentally ill! We've been talking about the problem all day. The problem is with your son's unblessed appendage.

AUGANBEK. Look, everything had been happily forgotten. So why bring this unpleasantness up again?

ABDASHIM. Wasn't it you who began this conversation yourselves? Where were you earlier? And you think of yourselves as close relatives! Where is your empathy? You're not even trying to cover up this mess, you want to discuss it further... Anything to create more gossip...

ISPANALI. Here he goes again, the infidel! If I were you I wouldn't make any accusations myself. Instead of admitting that it's his fault and keeping quiet, he's trying to stick his claws into us... He could at least look embarrassed. Even aksakal Rat is embarrassed...

ABDASHIM. The aksakal is at fault too – if he is the eldest among us, shouldn't he have enlightened us? At least remind us?

AUGANBEK. Of course!

ISPANALI. So what is this, you are getting us out of the way so that you can disrespect the aksakal? Shut your mouth you infidel!

ABDASHIM. I can't be an infidel – I have never once broken the laws of Sharia.

ISPANALI. You say you have never broken the laws? Then why don't you know how to read the Koran? Hasn't fifty years been enough?

ABDASHIM. Oh yes, and of course you're the perfect Muslim! You don't even wash your feet before you enter the mosque.

ISPANALI. Sometimes I do, sometimes I don't… Who are you to decide how clean I am? Do you also check whether I take a bucket of water into the latrine? Then you really are an infidel – bringing shame on yourself by not showing your son the righteous path!

AUGANBEK. Eh! What's the matter with you? Your face has already turned red from so much yelling! And for what? Stop this senseless quarrel!

ABDASHIM. I didn't start this quarrel, you did! You called me an imbecile, you said I was mentally ill. You called me an infidel!

ISPANALI. You don't read namaz *[Islamic prayers]*, you didn't get your son circumcised, you eat sausage, you drink vodka – who are you if not an infidel?

ABDASHIM. Eh, Ispanali! You're an expert at harassing people, too direct, even when a person doesn't want you to be... And here you are with your "infidel"! You know that her family lives on the other side of the railway tracks, with dozens of Russian families. They have nothing to do with circumcisions and namaz. But they also want to go to heaven. And they have such adorable children. And their girls are so beautiful…

At this moment aksakal Rat, who until then had been sitting in silence, joins the argument.

RAT. Imbeciles! What on earth do you think you are doing with all your senseless chattering? Did anyone ask you who goes to heaven and who goes to hell, who is beautiful and who is a shaitan [evil spirit]?

ABDASHIM. And if no-one asks, does that mean we can't say? How can we not be angry at those who called themselves atheists when they were working on the kolkhoz, then became mullahs as soon as the Party was gone? It's not for nothing that we have the saying "Sufis are devils who had nothing else to do".

RAT. That's already more than enough idle chatter. What do you think we should do now?

Silence.

ISPANALI. It's only a month until the bride arrives, what can we do? He's been walking around like this until now, so let him stay like this. Do you think someone is going to be spying on him? Atheism has to leave a trace of kindness too.

RAT. Stop joking around and get to the point!

AUGANBEK. Fine, I will get to the point: Bonaparte must be circumcised straight away. Today, at the very latest! This is the most correct decision to take.

ABDASHIM. Today? Oh my, and what if the boy doesn't agree to it?

AUGANBEK. He will agree to it. You will make him agree to it.

ABDASHIM. Oh my, but he isn't a small child – you can't just stroke his hair and tell him it isn't going to hurt. He's a grown jigit *[horseman]*! What if he grabs the knife out of the mullah's hands and stabs someone?

AUGANBEK. Then your job is to tie his hands and legs before you bring him to the mullah.

ABDASHIM. There is only a month until the wedding… What if he hasn't healed by then, what will we do?

AUGANBEK. Why wouldn't he heal – is someone going to put a curse on him? We had to go through this once as well, you know. It took a couple of days – three at most.

ABDASHIM. Once… We were young then…

ISPANALI. Why are we wasting our breath talking about this? What if it takes ten days, or fifteen? If you chopped his hand off it wouldn't take fifteen days to heal.

Auganbek, who had been sitting for a while lost in his own thoughts, smiling and rubbing his knee, suddenly gives a loud guffaw.

RAT. Have you lost your mind? What's wrong with you?!

AUGANBEK. We will never live this down…

RAT. With who?

AUGANBEK. With the bride. It'll be fine if he heals in time. But if he doesn't…

RAT. Enough of your stupid jokes! Unless you want to bring shame upon your family, let us get to work, starting today. Set up a yurt in the yard outside your home – we will make that son of yours presentable before lunchtime.

EVERYONE. – Yes!

We will do everything as you say.

Come on Abdashim, call your son…

ABDASHIM. I'm just thinking, will they let him leave his work?

ISPANALI. What, is he such a brilliant worker that they can't do without him for an afternoon? We can lift his car out of a ditch ourselves.

ABDASHIM. Then let's go…

Bektur appears again, with a newspaper in his hands.

BEKTUR. In accordance with the decision of a three-day meeting, and in order to obtain a detailed answer to the question "What needs to be done to facilitate the growth and prosperity of the village?" our representative Tasbolat, to whom we have all given money, has gone to Austria for personal talks with a soothsayer called Globa.

Bektur leaves again, but no-one pays much attention to him. They all look confused.

AUGANBEK. That poor man must have taken a real blow to the head…

ISPANALI. I don't think he was ever circumcised either.

Ultugan runs in, panting for breath.

ULTUGAN. My boy is nowhere to be seen! Someone saw him running towards the river, screaming "I'd rather drown than bring such shame upon myself!"

ISPANALI. Who saw him?

ULTUGAN. Churchill.

ISPANALI. Oh for goodness' sake! Come on, Auganbek! We need to find Bonaparte quickly and bring him here. And you, Abdashim, put up the yurt in the middle of the yard. Aksakal Rat, you can start sharpening your knife.

RAT. My knife is always ready.

ISPANALI. Listen, everyone! No-one apart from us can find out that Bonaparte is being circumcised.

ULTUGAN. So what can we tell the men he works with? They might ask...

ISPANALI. Tell them that he has fallen ill.

ABDASHIM. With what?

AUGANBEK. Does it matter? There are a lot of diseases to choose from. Say he has AIDS, or bird flu – just make sure no-one else sticks their nose in around here.

ABDASHIM. Bite that tongue of yours, Auganbek! You should be ashamed of yourself...

AUGANBEK. Eh, Abdashim, you could be a little more careful yourself. You have made your bed, now lie in it.

ABDASHIM. Insolence! You scoundrel! So now you have decided to mock me, have you? (*Abdashim throws himself at Auganbek*)

Auganbek and Ispanali laugh and run away.

***

Inside the yurt. Bonaparte is lying on a bed.
Auganbek and Ispanali enter.

AUGANBEK. How are you feeling?
Bonaparte is silent.
AUGANBEK. I asked you how you are feeling –
answer me!

Bonaparte merely gulps.

ISPANALI. How are you feeling, you worthless
dog?
BONAPARTE. I'm lying down, as you can see...
AUGANBEK. Yes, we can see that you are lying
down. How are you feeling?
BONAPARTE. How could I be feeling? I'm lying
down.
ISPANALI. Well, um... Do you feel any better?
BONAPARTE. I don't think so...
AUGANBEK. Eh, you have been in bed for two
weeks now! Why aren't you feeling better?
BONAPARTE. What do you want me to say?
ISPANALI. I don't think this waste of space even
wants to get better. There are only two weeks until his

bride arrives, and here he is in bed, without a care in the world!

AUGANBEK. It's no use just lying around, you need to try to get better.

BONAPARTE. How do I try to get better?

ISPANALI. Work it out for yourself! Or summon the spirits of your forefathers.

BONAPARTE. I already am summoning them.

AUGANBEK. Then do it better – you have to really want to.

BONAPARTE. Should I be involving my forefathers in such a shameful matter?

ISPANALI. Listen, I think he has a point here...

AUGANBEK. Or more likely he is just being cunning, and has found a way to lay around at home instead of going to work. It can't be taking so long to heal. It just isn't possible.

ISPANALI. You're right. His bed is made for him, the house is nice and cool, he has his meals brought to him on a tray... Let's have a look ourselves to see how he is healing...

AUGANBEK. How?

ISPANALI. Can you really not guess? Here, lift his blanket up. I'll take a look myself.

Auganbek takes the white blanket away from Bona-
parte and lifts it up. Ispanali goes around it to look at
what is underneath. Ultugan enters.

ULTUGAN. Oh my, what are you doing?

ISPANALI. Will you look at this scoundrel? The wound hasn't even closed! If he was one of us he would already be up and walking around – he must get his skin from his mother's genes.

ULTUGAN. Eh, and what do you have against his mother's genes? If he had taken after his mother he would be galloping like a stallion in three days. My dear Kazakhs, when are you going to stop blaming others for your own shortcomings?

ISPANALI *(Taken by surprise)* Oh, Auntie, when did you get here?

ULTUGAN. Does what you have to say about me depend on where I am? Praise God, his mother's genes are completely pure. Isn't that right? And rumour has it that once upon a time you also took more than two weeks to heal, so if you want to find defects, start by looking at yourself. All of our forefathers were mighty horsemen. One distant ancestor, Borykbai, suffered an injured arm in a battle and chopped it off himself, before killing about a hundred Jungar warriors.

BONAPARTE. Cool! You know, the Jungars had us under their yoke for two hundred years, but two of our ancestors managed to kill about three hundred of them…

AUGANBEK. Will you just listen to this helpless idiot? It's because of his stupid character that he has taken so long to heal.

BONAPARTE. What has my stupid character got to do with anything? I just wanted to ask you for a little less bragging, and a little more truth.

ISPANALI. Don't trouble your little head with the truth. First of all you need to think about getting better.

BONAPARTE. Thinking is no use…

ISPANALI. Well seeing as there is no use, you can get the hell out of here, can't you? If your bride finds out that you are here laying about, then she will probably die of shame.

BONAPARTE. So what are you telling me to do? I would rather have tied a rock to my neck and jumped in the river than go through all this shameful business – but you chased me on your horses, tied me up and dragged me to this bed. This is what happens when you force people to do things that they don't really want to do!

ISPANALI. It seems we have an audience with a philosopher! It would take a year to treat you of all of your ills, Bonaparte, my poor Frenchman!

ULTUGAN. Eh, you are going to exhaust my son with all of your chattering.

Ispanali suddenly laughs loudly.

ISPANALI. Just imagine if some real Frenchmen came here and saw a man called Bonaparte lying in such a state, in a little Kazakh village called Engels! Ha-ha-ha!

Voices in unison:

VOICES: – Everyone to the village club!

We're going to select the village akim [*head of local government*]!

Make sure everyone comes!

Our future is in your hands!

Everyone has to vote!

AUGANBEK. We chose an akim six months ago. What has happened there since?

ISPANALI. There are six parties working in our village. We are always holding meetings here for one of them or the other. Each party is trying to get its representative into power.

ULTUGAN. But none of these representatives ever settle in the village. The akim has changed six times in five years! People are confused, everything is in disarray.

AUGANBEK. The akims are to blame themselves. When they walk among us, like ordinary people, they have some clout – but as soon as they disappear, it's as if the previous akim was still in place.

ISPANALI. It's all because of democracy. As soon as that disaster happened to us, people just calmly stopped going to work.

BONAPARTE. Democracy is just a temporary mishap. The hurricane will run out of steam, and we'll all return to how things were.

ISPANALI. Oh really? Two weeks in bed reading newspapers and I see you've turned into an eminent politician. Listen, if lying around is doing you so much good then maybe you'd better stay here for another month! Or two… Or lay around for three months, then you can establish the Bonaparte Party and put yourself forward to be elected as akim. And if you'll be trying to become an akim, you won't need to get married…

ULTUGAN. As the saying goes, "It isn't the rider who notices the saddle chafing, but the horse – and it isn't a family that notices a worthy man, but the pas-

ser-by". Why are you all opening your mouths, if all that comes out is attacks and insults? Why not some kind words to lift the soul? Do you really think that my son is worse than anyone else? When he grows up he will show you what he is really made of. (*Ultugan strokes Bonaparte's head*).

AUGANBEK. Yes, Auntie, you are speaking God's truth. Bonaparte is still just a child. The poor boy has only just been circumcised...(*Auganbek tries to conceal his laughter*).

ULTUGAN. Laugh if you want to. But I'm warning you – he will show all of you. Our family has raised five sergeant majors, two judges, and one high sultan.

AUGANBEK. If you are from such a prestigious family, why did you marry our uncle Abdashim?

ULTUGAN. When the Soviets were in power no Kazakhs were registered as regal sons and daughters – we and our ancestors were cast as down-and-outs, no matter where we came from. But look at us today – none of us have poor roots: all of our ancestors were wealthy landowners, army men, horsemen, khans...

AUGANBEK. So Auntie, are you one of them?

ISPANALI. Listen, are we going to this meeting or not?

AUGANBEK. We can't miss it! If we do then those activists will just push another thief into power. But

where has our uncle Abdashim got to?

ULTUGAN. He left to go to the club a long time ago.

ISPANALI. But of course – he has to have his say at every meeting. He was so occupied with them that he forgot to have his son circumcised. (To Bonaparte). While we're gone, try not to fill your head with too many newspapers. Try summoning your mother's ancestors instead. Surely five sergeant majors, two judges and one high sultan will be able to help you?

ULTUGAN. You awful men, wagging your tongues instead of saying something nice!

Ultugan throws the chair she had been sitting on at Ispanali and Auganbek. They both run out of the room.

***

All members of the 'emergency committee' are in the
house: the aksakal Rat, Abdashim, Ultugan,
Ispanali and Auganbek.
There may be other people present,
but we don't need to name them.

ISPANALI. The situation is becoming more complicated, aksakal. There are only ten days until the relatives are introduced, and Bonaparte is still a long way from being healed.

RAT. Have you done everything I told you to do?

ABDASHIM. Everything, aksakal. The imam from the mouse came three times to read namaz. A young mullah also read from the Koran. For five days in a row a shaman blew the smoke from a white chicken onto him. We cut up a black ram, and gave the meat out to poor families. One night we took him to sleep next to the grave of a sacred pilgrim. Three times after midnight we shot our weapons outside the house. To make sure that there was always food on the table, we ate almost all of the food that we had bought for the wedding.

ULTUGAN. Are mullahs these days turning into businessmen? Don't take another step towards the patient…

Aksakal Rat gives Ultugan a disapproving glance.

ABDASHIM. Look, everyone – the words of our aksakal are the most important. People have only ever accepted his advice with words of gratitude.

AUGANBEK. I suppose it couldn't hurt to take him to the doctor?

ULTUGAN. Does this village have even one slightly competent doctor? The hospital went to pieces a long time ago. The only person there now is a young lad, and he doesn't know his arse from his elbow.

AUGANBEK. They say he isn't even a doctor. When he gives you an injection the needle goes all the way through your arm and out the other side.

ISPANALI. He was hired by activists from the "Tauekel" party at the last meeting!

AUGANBEK. But the party "Praise to God" is on their case – if their candidate becomes the village's akim then he will be straight over to the hospital. It's promises that win elections!

ULTUGAN. To hell with all of them! While they're trying to become akims you get headaches from their promises. People are tired of these scoundrels.

ABDASHIM. You know, I went to see that doctor the other day. He barked at me: "Whoever did your son's circumcision, get him to treat it. If you had asked me to do it he would be fine by now. It's your ignorance that has done all this!" Then he threw me out!

AUGANBEK. He's a wise man…

Auganbek gives a hearty laugh. Ispanali joins in.
Abdashim and Ultugan follow suit.

RAT. This is not a time to be laughing! Eh, you, layabouts and bickerers, laughing about matters like these is sinful!

ISPANALI. Aksakal, don't be so harsh – they say that laughing at silly pieces of gossip lightens the soul. Ever since that man-child has been circumcised, we, his relatives, have taken on all of his work.

Abdashim is also doing everything that he can. Ky-dy-ata is always unhappy with us about something, but the treatments we have tried on Bonaparte haven't had any effect. Our failures are due to ecology – I think it's because the air is polluted!

RAT. It's your conscience that is polluted. Your conscience!

ABDASHIM. I don't remember ever wishing anyone ill, or doing anything even a tiny bit malicious. So I don't understand why we are being subjected to all this abuse.

RAT. It isn't only you. Everyone sitting here is to blame. Everyone – the whole village! The whole district! If all that you have said is a lie; if you read the Koran over a dastarkhan, where bad water and bad food are placed together; if such words as sin and beneficence are completely forgotten; if so many ignorant mullahs have appeared… then how can the whole planet not be overtaken by evil and sabotage? Punishment! Punishment! This too is punishment! This is the answer God has sent down to us!

Rat leaves, without looking at anyone.
Everyone is silent.

ISPANALI. So what are we going to do?

AUGANBEK. What do you mean?

ISPANALI. There are only ten days until we have to receive the bride. So what are we going to do?

AUGANBEK. Within ten days that charlatan will be able to drive there and back!

ISPANALI. And if he can't?

AUGANBEK. Then… Then you will be the groom and you'll drive there instead.

ISPANALI. What?! Have you lost your mind? How can I be the groom?

AUGANBEK. Easy! We will give you a wash and a shave, and dress you up.

ISPANALI. And if they realise that they are being deceived?

AUGANBEK. They won't. We will leave at night, and come back at night too. Luckily the electricity in their village has gone off. Someone stole their cable.

ISPANALI. Are you being serious? The bride's friends and aunts will want to go through the groom's pockets, and lay a meal out for him. We aren't going to be sitting in the dark not able to see each other.

AUGANBEK. Then don't look at anyone, keep your head down. Don't talk, and don't laugh too loudly. All you have to do is smile.

ISPANALI. So you want everyone to think there is something wrong with the groom? Then you can go yourself. You're three years younger than me. And you look more like Bonaparte than I do.

AUGANBEK. No, no, I can't!

ISPANALI. Why not?

AUGANBEK. Because one of my wives is from that village. And the other one has relatives there. They will recognise me there straight away!

ISPANALI. Of all the villages in Kazakhstan to get your wives from...

AUGANBEK. You talk as if he only looked in one village...

ISPANALI. And it's still giving us headaches…

Our old friend Bektur enters.
As before his head is buried in a newspaper.
He reads aloud and pays no attention to anyone.

BEKTUR. The Chinese government, just 70-80 kilometres from the border with Kazakhstan, conducted a second test of a 55-kiloton nuclear weapon at the Lobnor test site. The Kazakh government and the Semey-Nevada movement did not issue any warning to the Chinese authorities!

Bektur leaves.

AUGANBEK *(Glancing at Bektur)*. Eh, we have enough to worry about as it is, we don't need another problem. Get out of here!

ISPANALI. That poor man really needs to be seriously treated. As soon as we have Bonaparte's wedding out of the way, we'll turn our attention to that poor moron.

AUGANBEK. Well, what do you suggest? Are you going to be a groom for the day, or have you got a better idea?

ISPANALI. Ten years ago my distant cousin Tazakulu had a bride brought home to him. That day he had got drunk, and ended up sleeping it off in a police cell, so I took her into the house instead of him. So what now, do you want me to do the same again?

AUGANBEK. Well, since you have some experience...

ISPANALI. So am I the replacement groom for everyone in this village? No, no-one is going to believe me again, I'm not doing it!

AUGANBEK. Eh, let's have another look at Bonaparte. It's just impossible that he still can't get up.

ISPANALI. Let's give the patient some peace.

***

Inside the yurt. Bonaparte is on the bed, reading a newspaper. Auganbek and Ispanali enter.

ISPANALI. So, pea-brain, any change?

Bonaparte doesn't reply.

AUGANBEK. He doesn't even look at us. He could at least have said hello.
Silence.

ISPANALI. If this week you can't get your useless body out of bed, Your Imperial Highness, then one of us will go and fetch your bride. What do you think of that, Your Highness?
More silence.

AUGANBEK. Just look at this pea-brain, lying around without a care in the world! And making us do all his work for him! I think his bed rest has turned him into a real sloth. But it's no surprise: his relatives on his mother's side were lazy as well.

Ultugan enters. She hears what Auganbek says.

ULTUGAN. His relatives on his mother's side did an honest day's work and went to bed with a clear conscience. The ones who rushed around from morning till night getting nothing done came from your side of the family.

ISPANALI. Auntie, when will you stop listening in on every word we say? How long have you been here for? And where is our uncle Abdashim?

ULTUGAN. He's on the list, so he can't get away.

AUGANBEK. What list?

ULTUGAN. Your uncle wants to become an akim. He has put himself up for the elections.

ISPANALI. The elections? He wants to be an akim?

ULTUGAN. Eh, what's so surprising about that? Or do you think that Abdashim doesn't have the brains for it?

ISPANALI. How could we say something like that about our own relative?

But… well… he did finish school after the seventh grade...

ULTUGAN. You don't need an education to become a boss. In the old times the warriors didn't go

to institutes and colleges like you, and they still ruled over people.

ISPANALI. That was a different time...

AUGANBEK. Eh, you... Some were station chiefs, some were workers' committees, when you were recommended for election you flatly refused, proudly saying 'we have our own work to do'...

ISPANALI. The boy laying in front of us also wants to become an akim. What is wrong with people? They don't even care whether they are able to govern people or not. They just don't care!

ULTUGAN. And that young mullah who came twice last week to read Bonaparte an incantation... The one who took three thousand tenge from us... He's also trying to become an akim.

AUGANBEK. Lord, forgive us! This is what people mean when they say "Be patient, Kazakh – you'll become an ataman [*Cossack leader*]!"

ULTUGAN. Cossack, not Kazakh, you idiot!

AUGANBEK. What's the difference? They sound almost the same! And by the way, Kazakhs were Cossacks once...

ULTUGAN. Your uncle has decided that he isn't going to get enough votes. He's asking me to call both of you to help him.

AUGANBEK. Well, honorary son-in-law, shall we go?

ISPANALI. Let's resolve this problem first, then we'll see.

AUGANBEK. There's nothing to see – there's no point in going! Let them elect who they want. There isn't a single worthy man among them anyway.

ULTUGAN. I should be ashamed to call you a relative!

ISPANALI. Eh, Auntie – why do you get so cross at everything I say? Think about it – what does Abdashim need to be an akim for? Don't we already have enough problems? His son is lying here useless, not even able to talk. You'd be better off calling Abdashim back here. There is an urgent matter to attend to!

ULTUGAN. (*Gently stroking her son's hair*). Oh, my darling, I would do anything for you! I'm going to bring you a bowl of yummy soup.

Ultugan leaves quickly.

ISPANALI. Put those newspapers down! (*He rips them out of Bonaparte's hands*). What is it with this endless rest? Say something at least!

BONAPARTE. What can I say? You have all managed to say everything without me.

AUGANBEK. Listen, what on earth is a hot water bottle doing here? (*He takes the hot water bottle from under the blanket*).

BONAPARTE. It's water...

AUGANBEK. If it's water then why are you hiding it under your blanket? (*He unscrews the top of the bottle and takes a sniff. He sniffs again, then tastes a drop of the liquid*). Eh, isn't this vodka? What is this, are you lying here and swigging vodka?

BONAPARTE. Well, the jigits brought it for me. They said it would help me to heal...

ISPANALI. Well I never! His breath smells of alcohol!

BONAPARTE. Um… well… All the same while I'm lying here I have nothing to do…

AUGANBEK. So now we know! And here was I wondering how he had turned into such an avid reader. It turns out he was trying to hide the smell... With 'medicine' like this you're not going to heal even in a year, have you got that?! (*He takes one swig of the vodka, then a bigger one*). You idiot! What moron do you have to be to keep vodka in a hot water bottle?

ISPANALI. Is it really vodka? Give it here (*He takes a small sip, then two big ones*). Well, if you're going to lie here drunk all day then you'll never get better! You're a drunk!

AUGANBEK. Your daddy is loitering around at the club, and here you are lazing around here! (*He takes two more sips from the hot water bottle*).

ISPANALI. What a sage our aksakal Rat was – he obviously has a nose for these things. Remember what he said – where there is vodka, angels will never fly… (*He also takes the bottle and takes two sips*).

AUGANBEK. And who's bringing you the vodka?

BONAPARTE. Churchill and Roosevelt.

AUGANBEK. Ah yes – you are drinking in esteemed company! Tomorrow we're going to start changing all of your names. It has to be done. . What idiocy, that Kazakhs don't have enough names of their own…

BONAPARTE. What name are you going to choose?

ISPANALI. It's all our own fault... Auganbek, come here, let's sing together!

> *At that moment Bonaparte's little
> brother Chapai enters.*

CHAPAI. Uncle Auganbek! Kashpirovsky's show is going to be on the television in an hour. Our whole village is going to watch it. They have even postponed the meeting at the club until tomorrow.

ISPANALI. Where is your father, if he isn't collecting the keys to the akim's office?

CHAPAI. They are also coming here. They told me to run here so you would have time to get ready.

AUGANBEK. Fine, we'll get ready. 'I have seen everything now' a woman once said, as she got ready to get married for the sixth time.

ISPANALI. By the way, you need to bring the television here and switch it on.

CHAPAI. There is no plug here. We need to go into the big house.

ISPANALI. Get up then, Sir Bonaparte. We are going to marvel at a hypnotist called Kashpirovsky. Perhaps he will free us from our own little ailments. Auganbek, help Sir Bonaparte to walk.

As music plays, Kashpirovsky opens his show.

KASHPIROVSKY. I'm not going to give names to your sicknesses. The magical power held inside my words will search for and find everything that is making you ill. A person's organism is made up of a special energy that we ourselves don't understand. I will awaken the source of this energy. The awoken energy will find any form of sickness and fight it by itself. During this show, try not to think about anything – you can

even forget about your pains. You can think about me anything you like. I don't pay attention to such things. This is because I wish you only good things. And now you are falling into a pleasant dream and starting to fall asleep...

Either Kashpirovsky's soothing voice made them sleepy, or the alcohol had gone to their heads, but Auganbek and Ispanali's heads begin to drop, as they struggle to stay awake.

I'm giving an order. One, two, three, four...

AUGANBEK. (*With difficulty lifting his head*). Well? Is it working?

BONAPARTE. I don't know...

ISPANALI. As usual, then – you don't know. If you don't know then do I have to know?

AUGANBEK. Just relax and lie down!

ISPANALI. Don't be shy. We are all men here. Let Kashpirovsky see... Get it out and lie down!

KASHPIROVSKY. The healing of any illness depends on faith. If you genuinely believe, then my blessed words can work wonders from a thousand kilometres away. They hold the power of faith, the power of conviction. I believe you. I love you. I don't sleep at

night, thinking about your health. Yes, I can feel that you are relaxed now. Close your eyes. Sleep soundly... Dream on, float free in the blue skies of your imagination... And now I will begin to wake you up. I'll count to ten: one, two, three, four...

AUGANBEK. Well, Bonaparte, do you feel any changes?

Bonaparte is silent.

Eh, he's already snoring! Let's take him back to his bed.

ISPANALI. Good grief, his father is snoring too! Abdashim, the show's over, you can get up.

ABDASHIM. (*In his sleep*). For the party "Tau-ekel"! Only forward!

ISPANALI. (*Laughing loudly*) Oh, stupid uncle of mine, what does politics need with you? They are both better off in bed.

Ultugan enters.

ULTUGAN. So, is there any hope he'll get better?

AUGANBEK. There is, Auntie, there is. Our little darling is fast asleep. God must have decided to lend a hand. While we carry these two, put them to bed and come back, then put out the dastarkhan. It's time it saw a feast!

ULTUGAN. Have you ever seen our dastarkhan empty? Everything is already prepared, over there in the part of the house where the women sit!

ISPANALI. Well done, Auntie! You must come from a worthy family after all!

Both leave, supporting one another.

ABDASHIM. (*Still sleep-talking*). Long live the party "Praise to God"!

AUGANBEK. Long live it indeed!

***

A large stage. This could be Abdashim's house, but we don't have to explain where events are taking place. People are talking worriedly about something.

VOICES. – People, calm down!

–Tasbolat has returned from Austria.

– He will tell us all what the future holds for us.

– Oh my, we have been waiting for this for years. Does this village have a future?

– Here he is, let's welcome him. Here is the Tasbolat who has met and received an audience with the clairvoyant Globa!

– Wonderful!

– Tasbolat, welcome home! So tell us, what will our future be like?

TASBOLAT. The future will be good. The economy will pick up, incomes will grow, and life will be happier.

VOICES. – Your wishes will come true!

– This is music to our ears!

– What do we have to do? What did Globa say?

TASBOLAT. He said that we need to work.

VOICES. – He said what?

– What did you say?

– Say it again!

TASBOLAT. He said that we need to work.

VOICES. – Idiot!

– Cretin!

– We collected all that money to send you all that way... and that's all you found out?

– We don't need Globa to tell us we need to work!

– He should give us our money back!

– Just listen to this! Idiot! Cretin! Get him out of here!

– We should take him into the desert and leave him there!

The angry crowd lunges at Tasbolat. Tasbolat runs into the steppe. Everyone runs after him. Only Auganbek, Ispanali, Abdashim and Ultugan remain.

ABDASHIM. This is the end of the world! It's as if everyone has lost their mind!

AUGANBEK. It's not the end of the world. Everything is as it used to be. This is all our own fault.

ISPANALI. It isn't about whether Tasbolat went to see Globa or not. But there is something in what he said.

ULTUGAN. To hell with your meeting, and your Globa. Is my boy getting enough rest?

Just then someone resembling a bear walks in.
Everyone goes silent and freezes in fright.

AUGANBEK. Ah, it's… the village doctor, Rollan. Good evening!

ISPANALI. What are you doing here so late?

ULTUGAN. Come in, young man, come in…

ROLLAN. Which one of you called me a veterinarian?

In a crescendo:

– Why would we say something like that?! Heaven help us!

– May we all fall down with bird flu!

ROLLAN. Everyone should mind his own business. Don't you all go around spreading rumours, or I'll take this needle and put you all to sleep, have you got that?

ALL IN UNISON: – Of course! Got it!

– We understand!

ROLLAN. When they did the circumcision, some microbes got in. Even a third-rate vet would understand that. Your Bonaparte will get better. I've been coming here three days in a row, at night, to clean his

wounds with medical spirit. Bonaparte! Come here and show yourself to your family and friends!

Bonaparte enters, wearing a white gown.
Everyone embraces him.

ULTUGAN. Is this real or am I dreaming? Oh my, doctor, my good young man, come and sit with us, have something to eat, I made this all myself.

ROLLAN. I don't have time now. I will come another time.

ABDASHIM. If you want you can come with us to bring the bride home..

ROLLAN. I have some bad news for you. Your son's future father-in-law has found out about your little misfortune, and out of shame has made a run for it in the direction of Syr-Darya!

VOICES. – Made a run for it? How?

– Our shame has caught up with us after all! This is the end of us!

– How are we going to look people in the eye?!

– Never mind that, how are we going to get our dowry back? We've already paid for half of it…

ROLLAN. It appears the girl was a strong one. She couldn't stand the shame, she ran away and tried to throw herself in the river with a rock around her

neck. But two people caught up with her on horses and dragged her home. It sounds like she is still locked up in the house..

ULTUGAN. Well what do you expect, the poor girl has been through the same torture as our son. At least God stopped the disaster from happening!

AUGANBEK. You could say that both of them share the same fate. Love between people so young burns hotter than any fire...

ABDASHIM. But tell us, what must we do now?

ROLLAN. Show your slavish obedience, go and fall at their feet. Maybe they will forgive you..

ABDASHIM. And we won't have to do anything else?

ROLLAN. No, just be healthy!

The two say farewell to each other.
Then everyone surrounds Bonaparte,
looking him up and down.

AUGANBEK. Come on, show us how you can walk...

Bonaparte takes a couple of steps.

ISPANALI. Now jump!

Bonaparte climbs onto a chair and jumps off.

AUGANBEK. Not bad, Bonaparte! It wasn't for nothing that you spent the best part of a month laying in bed. (*To Ispanali*) And are you still sure that you're not going to play the replacement groom again?

ISPANALI. No chance! God will spare me…

AUGANBEK. Let's take our horses for a ride around the village tomorrow, what do you say, Bonaparte?

BONAPARTE. As you wish…

ABDASHIM. And what about the meeting tomorrow?

ISPANALI. Tomorrow you, aksakal Rat and I are going to hunt down that girl's father, fall at his feet and beg him to forgive us. You can forget about any meeting!

ULTUGAN. I'll go and pack you a bag.

Once again Bektur suddenly appears, and gives a speech to no-one in particular.

BEKTUR. The Baltimore City Court in the United States ordered the imprisonment for life of a Kazakh girl, Galiya Asanova, on false accusations of involvement in a murder. The Kazakh side did not even

try to influence the course of the judicial investigation. Public organisations and representatives of the intelligentsia also silently ignored this decision. Wake up, Kazakh! Wake up, Kazakh!

He leaves.

ISPANALI. That man only ever appears when we are in the middle of a drama.

ULTUGAN. I told you that a brick fell on his head.

AUGANBEK. So let him go back to where it happened. What is he bothering us for? And what does he mean with all this "Wake up, Kazakh"?

Does he think we're sleeping?

ABDASHIM. I think he's just a bit simple. Maybe he is really the holy Kydyr-ata, who walks across the world's lands and oceans...

AUGANBEK. What holy man is going to appear at a time like this? They have probably long since disappeared from the face of the earth.

ABDASHIM. Still, it's worth thinking about...

ISPANALI. It's worth thinking about something else. Are we going to look for this girl's father tomorrow or not?

ABDASHIM. We've already agreed about that.

AUGANBEK. So, Bonaparte, son of Abdashim! Are you ready to take yourself a bride?

BONAPARTE. That girl from before?

AUGANBEK. What are you talking about, that girl from before? Do you really not care which one it is?

BONAPARTE. Of course I care!

AUGANBEK. Then why are you talking nonsense like that? Let's prepare for tomorrow's journey!

***

The same cheerful music plays as it did at the beginning. Bonaparte's younger brother Chapai runs around the stage.

CHAPAI. Hooray! It's decided! Uncle Bonaparte is bringing his bride home tomorrow! Everyone is invited to the wedding! Come one, come all! Come and share our joy with us! There will be singing and dancing! Everybody come to the wedding!

END

www.ingramcontent.com/pod-product-compliance
Lightning Source LLC
Chambersburg PA
CBHW070011100426
42741CB00012B/3196